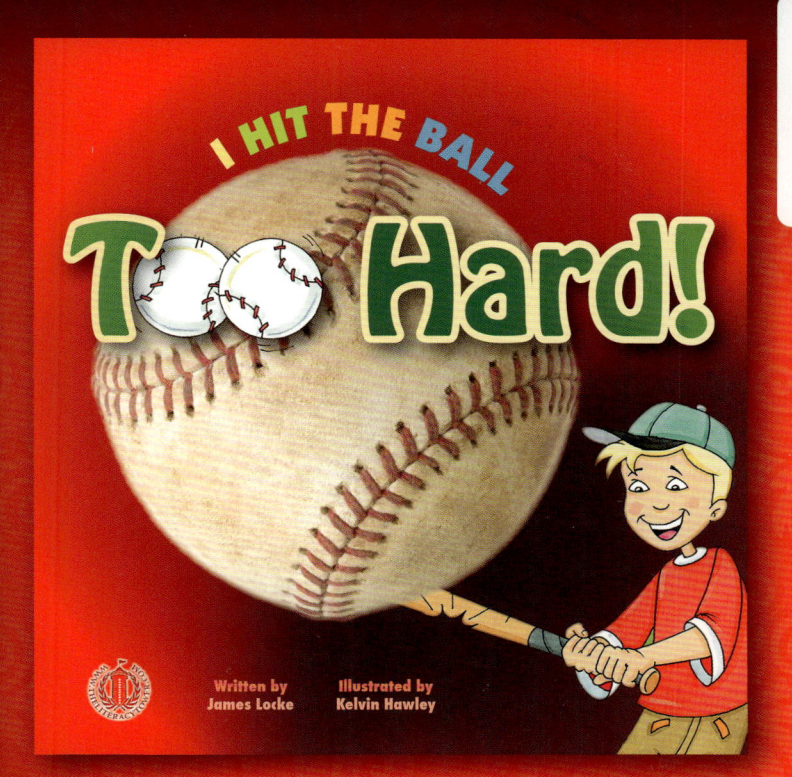

I HIT THE BALL Too Hard!

Written by James Locke
Illustrated by Kelvin Hawley

"What do you think will happen when a boy hits the ball too hard?"

Grusilda xxx

a boy

a ball

a window

Today I hit the ball for the first time.

I am happy because
I hit the ball hard.

But I hit the ball *too* hard.

Where will the ball fall down?

The ball started to fall down by an old house.

The ball went through
the window of the old house.

Now we have to go next door and say sorry!